RUGBY FOR KIDS

SEBASTIÁN E. PERASSO

RUGBY FOR KIDS

Translated by
Florencia Ferraris

CLUB HOUSE

Perasso, Sebastián E.
  Rugby for kids / Sebastián E. Perasso. - 1a ed . - Ciudad Autónoma de Buenos Aires : Deldragón, 2019.
  116 p. ; 22,86 x 15,24 cm.

  Traducción de: Florencia Ferraris.

  1. Deportes para Niños. 2. Rugby. I. Ferraris, Florencia, trad. II. Título.
  CDD 796.333

CLUB HOUSE *Publishers*
Un sello de Ediciones Deldragón
Emilio Mitre 71 – 7º B (1424) Buenos Aires
República Argentina

RUGBY FOR KIDS

© 2019, Sebastián E. Perasso

Dirección editorial: Ricardo J. Sabanes
Traducción al inglés: Florencia Ferraris
Diseño: Laura Restelli

Derechos de edición reservados para todo el mundo:
© 2019, Ediciones Deldragón

Primera edición: febrero 2019

edicionesdeldragon@gmail.com
www.edicionesdeldragon.com.ar

Queda hecho el depósito que prevé la ley 11.723
Impreso en la Argentina

Ninguna parte de esta publicación, incluido el diseño de la cubierta, puede ser reproducida, almacenada o transmitida en manera alguna ni por ningún medio, ya sea eléctrico, químico, mecánico, óptico, de grabación o de fotocopia, sin permiso previo del editor.

TABLE OF CONTENTS

Dedication	7
Thanks	9
Foreword	11
Introduction	13

CHAPTER 1 – THE HISTORY OF RUGBY

Before rugby	19
The origins of rugby	24
The evolution of rugby	30
Rugby Expands	35

CHAPTER 2 – GETTING TO KNOW RUGBY

The aim of the game	45
Little oval dictionary	48
Knowing the laws	58
Technical handbook	62
Developing good habits	77
The principles of the game	78
Safety	84

CHAPTER 3 – GUARDIANS OF THE GAME

The spirit of rugby	89
The true sportsperson	92
My behaviour	95
15 tips for the player	100
The 10 reasons of a team	102

CHAPTER 4 – WINNING AND LOSING

Winning	107
Losing	108

EPILOGUE

Chasing our dreams	113

*To the little boys and girls that play
rugby all around the world.
This is my small tribute
to all of them.*

THANKS

Writing an eight book on rugby in less than ten years inevitably means getting in a dangerous whirlwind. I do not think anything I have achieved in the world of writing would have been possible without the support of my wife and my children. They know of my strong vocation for rugby and give me the support I need.

To Monic, Isidro and Faustina, my eternal appreciation.

FOREWORD

By Diego Albanese *

It fills me with pride that Sebastián (or Cheba, as his friends from San Isidro Club and many others know him) has invited me to write some words for his book *RUGBY FOR KIDS*.

There is something I believe that connects us, and this is how crazy we both are about this game, this wonderful sport, rugby, which, in my opinion, is the best and most complete of all.

And why do I call it complete? Because rugby is much more than a sport, it is much more than running, tackling, pushing, kicking, rucking… Rugby educates you, teaches you, shapes you, and forms your character.

Nowadays, as a father, I long for my children, their friends, and as many kids as possible to get close to the oval ball so that they can live and experience everything that this game provides over time.

Being part of a team, being generous towards our teammates, accepting the referee's authority, obeying the coach's decisions, respecting the opponent, being punctual, making sacrifices… are only part of the essence of this fantastic sport. Thet are experiences from which we prepare for life itself.

And the best thing, and what makes it even more complete, is that there is a place for everyone in rugby. It is the only sport played by short, tall, brawny, slim, slow, and fast people. Yes, everyone. Everyone plays, everyone is important, and no one can do anything if they don't have fourteen mates around them.

For this reason, if you had any doubts, the moment you hold Cheba's book in your hands and you read it, you won't hesitate to give rugby a try. You won't regret it!

To finish, I leave a great statement that a coach said to me when I was a boy and that I have carried with me ever since:

> **When the right wing scores a try, congratulate the loose head prop who pushed to get the ball.**

That is rugby.

Have a good game! Enjoy it!

---

*Diego Albanese played for San Isidro Club from Buenos Aires, and later in France an England. He won 55 caps with Los Pumas.

INTRODUCTION

Dear kids, I want to tell you something. Almost ten years ago, I wrote my first book on rugby. And from that moment on, I felt the need to recount in paper all my rugby experiences, apart from all those lessons I have been learning along the years.

My father took me to play rugby when I was very small. He was the coach of the First XV of my club, SIC, and also the Pumas, the Argentinian national rugby team, and this allowed me to learn from him, while having the opportunity to surround myself with coaches and players who deeply love this game.

These fanaticism and passion for rugby were passed down to me from my social and family circles. I have always believed – and I still do – that I have been in a truly privileged place to learn since I was very young. That is why I thought that I could make a contribution to rugby by writing.

But it was not only about revealing what I had learnt from my elders, because I understood that I should complete my education by studying everything that has to do with rugby. This stage of analysis and detailed study was necessary for me to complete my preparation.

This last bit was not difficult because my great curiosity led me to study every aspect of the game and, from there, I dealt with the analysis of many interesting topics: the technical, the tactical, and the psychological aspects of the player; the roles or purposes of the coach; the history of rugby, he values and traditions of the game, as well as the world of age grade rugby and its special characteristics.

I confess that I have always been very disciplined. And when it came to writing, I have dedicated a lot of time, energy, and determination.

This is something that gives me a lot of happiness and satisfaction. How nice it is that one can save a part of the day to do what one likes!

However, apart from my wild drive for writing, it is also true that the people who read my books gave me the necessary energy to quickly advance in the road of writing. That way, almost like magic, when I stopped to think about it, there were already six books of my authorship in my bookcase...

But I will tell you a secret. I have not read them again, although I sometimes flick through them. Not because I am not interested in my work, but because I feel that when one period has ended, another must necessarily open.

It is not good to stand still watching what we have done, as we would be looking at the past too much and neglecting something as valuable and important as the present. We need to set goals and challenges for ourselves each day because that is what moves us and creates enthusiasm in us.

How boring would life be if we did not have any goal! Having goals is the opposite of being adrift.

Today, a decade after I started writing on rugby, I did not want to forget about you, who are the future of the game and the most valuable treasure.

I hope you enjoy this book as much as I have enjoyed writing it. I invite you to get into this fabulous sport called rugby, assured that by practising it, you will become better athletes than before and – at the same time – better people.

CHAPTER 1
THE HISTORY OF RUGBY

BEFORE RUGBY

Rugby as you know it today has not always been like this.

In the old days, there were some games played with a ball that were direct precedents to our rugby. We have to go back many centuries to look for its most remote origins.

Historians agree that some of rugby's old relatives may be the Greek *episkyros*, the Roman *harpastum,* and the *Soule*, a game the French played around 1000 AD.

The history of Greece tells us that the ball was used in several sports. Many centuries back, the Greek created something called *episkyros* and it consisted in throwing and kicking a ball. Although it is a sport which we know little about, historians believe it had certain special features, like being practised by naked men and women, who were covered in aromatic oils.

Episkyros

In its beginnings, the ball was made of linen and hair strung together. This ball did not bounce so much, which is why they soon started using balls made from inflated pigs' bladders, which were wrapped with pig or deer leather.

Harpastum was a sport practised by the Romans since the first century. It is also known as "the game with the small ball," as records from that era point out that the size and hardness of the ball was similar to a baseball.

Although records are limited and there are some contradictory opinions regarding certain regulations, the game took place in a rectangular field divided in two, with teams of players who could dodge each other and throw passes.

Each team stood on one half of the field. That half was their turf, and the goal of the game was to pass the ball among each other without giving the rival team a chance to steal it. Each team had to maintain the ball in their half for as long as possible, while the opponents would try to prevent this by stealing the ball and taking it to their own side.

Few accounts say that the objective of the game was to score points, passing the ball through the limit line of the rival's territory, similar to rugby, until the goal was reached, which is the same as "crossing enemy lines."

To steal the ball, the opponent could tackle, but unlike in rugby, high tackles were allowed!

Harpastum

An important rule of *harpastum* that coincides with rugby said that only the ball carrier could be tackled. This restriction encouraged the development of many passes and game strategies. Thanks to this, the players established specific rules for the game, as well as several tricks and different tactics.

It is also known that there have been some games which hundreds of players took part of.

It was an incredibly fast sport of great physical exhaustion that involved speed, agility, and physical effort.

In a time of constant wars and armed conflicts, *harpastum* was played to entertain and keep the healthy physical conditions of the Roman soldiers.

Besides, the game of *harpastum* was an occasion for the army to develop their fighting spirits because, just like rugby, *harpastum* shaped character.

However, sometimes the game got too violent and some men were gravely injured and could even die.

Emperor Julius Caesar was a big fan and promoter of this game, and he encouraged its practice between battles.

So magnetic was *harpastum* among the Romans that the emperors after Julius Caesar included it as part of the military training. Roman campaigns used to last several years, and sport was a way to entertain and motivate the troops. Due to the extension of the Roman Empire, the soldiers spread *harpastum* all over the places they conquered.

In Gaul, the old France, the game which was practised had some similarities to rugby and football. This game was called *la Soule*.

La Soule was a ball game that basically consisted in carrying the ball from one side of the town to the other by running. This route was interrupted with fights between both sides when they battled for the ball.

The instrument of the game could be a leather ball, a pig's bladder, a wooden ball, or a fabric ball.

The rules tended to change a lot. However, the kick-off always was in a fixed spot (a park, the town cemetery, etc.).

Authorities were against the practice of this sport because they deemed it too violent. That is why it was met with fierce resistance from some sectors.

An ordinance for King Charles I of France on 3 April 1365 makes up one of the oldest documents that give account of the practice of this discipline.

In 1440, an interdiction by the Bishop of Tréguier threatened the people who played this game with fines and even excommunication.

In the 15th century, *la Soule* was forbidden in France due to its violent nature.

La soule

THE ORIGIN OF RUGBY

Its beginnings

Throughout the years, the discussion surrounding the origins of rugby has always been present.

Legends says that one November afternoon in 1823, an English student from a public school in the city of Rugby, during a football match, took the ball in his arms and ran with it, giving rise to the game of rugby. This young boy was named William Webb Ellis. The Rugby World Cup celebrated every four years since 1987 was named after him to pay homage.

Young William's movement did not go unnoticed at all, since it planted the seed for this wonderful sport.

Statue of William Webb Ellis

From there, many students started practising rugby in that school and then, in other English schools and universities.

This story-legend is a mixture of fiction and reality, but the truth is that Rugby School is where this adventure called rugby begins, named this way in honour of that English school where everything started.

William Webb Ellis was born on 24 November 1806 in the city of Salford, England. And although he is considered the inventor of rugby, once he left Rugby School, he never had contact with this sport again.

In 1825, two years after that unforgettable afternoon, he got into Oxford University, where he would become a distinguished cricket player.

William Webb Ellis' feat is commemorated by a plaque on the fields of Rugby School that reads:

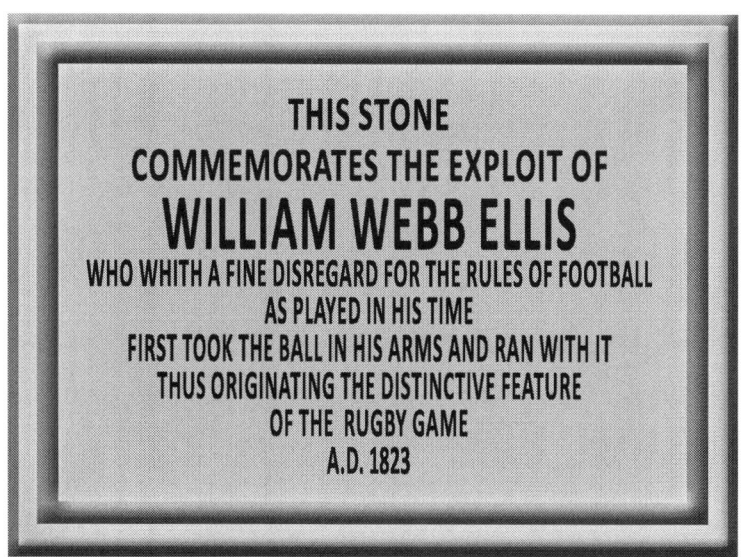

Commemorative plaque at Rugby School

Thomas Arnold, the transmitter

But beyond that run, a mixture of rebellion, lucidity, and inspiration, nothing would have been possible without the tireless endeavour of headmaster Thomas Arnold. Thanks to his work, rugby rose both in number of supporters and in public esteem.

The game started by Ellis could not have transformed by its own the sports of that time, nor could it have produced the deep changes that were made in that period with the appearance of rugby.

The architect of the developing and spreading of the game was *Thomas Arnold*.

After educating university students for almost a decade, he started working as a headmaster in Rugby School between 1828 and 1841. His strong religious beliefs made him completely transform the institution's pedagogy, building a different model from those in other schools. Arnold welcomed sports as an effective means for the players to become good Christians. This way, he used rugby as a vehicle to achieve his purposes and goals.

From his place, he managed to bring a true educational revolution in a period characterised by the disregard towards rules and poor discipline.

His reform in education gained such prestige and fame that it was adopted by the English state. From then on, many other countries adhered to these methods.

Rugby has always been a school of values!

New laws

> Due to rugby's growth in popularity, those who practised it found themselves with the obligation to regulate the game. The students of Rugby School made it official as a game when they implemented some rules in 1845. On 25 August that same year, three students between sixteen and eighteen years of age called William Delafield Arnold (son of headmaster Thomas Arnold), W. W. Shirley, and Frederick Hutchins received the order to write up the rules of the football played at Rugby School, representing a committee of eight students who were in charge of establishing them. Three days later, after being approved by a student assembly, the first rules of the game were published as *The Laws of Football as Played at Rugby School*. These first written rules were later adopted by different schools and universities, helping to turn a school game into a global sporting phenomenon.

Conflicting opinions

At the time, rugby football generated different opinions inside English schools.

In some followers it created feelings of enthusiasm and fanaticism, while in some others it brought out certain rejection and disapproval.

To understand the sector of society that opposed the practice of rugby, it would be good to do a little review on football in that period.

At that time, players could push the ball with any part of their bodies and had to get it to the end line of the rival's turf. The ball could be carried forward in any way, and could even be grabbed with the hands, although only to stop it and then kick it.

Kicking and tripping opponents up (always below the knees) was allowed, and many times players ended up in scrummages (scrums), battling for the ball.

Bigger and stronger players called battle horses were in charge of that task.

At the same time, those who waited to get the ball and run with it until the opposite goal line were called the light brigade.

Once rugby is born and spreads, there were many sectors opposed to the change, who put up a strong resistance because they thought the students committed to this sport would lose courage and manliness.

THE EVOLUTION OF RUGBY

In its beginnings, rugby was practised with the same ball as football, in giant fields and between hundreds of players in each team.

It is strange that only by 1850 was the round ball replaced by the oval one, made from a pig's bladder, inflated and covered with a leather wrapping.

The first clubs

The growth of rugby brought along the creation of the first clubs, which inherited from the English schools the passion for the game.

Much has been discussed about which one is the oldest club in the world. Some argue it is Barnes Rugby Football Club, from 1839, but the fact that there is no documentation to back this weakens this version.

Some records from that period say that Guy's Hospital Rugby Club was founded in 1843 in the City of Southwark, England. A card from 1883 that refers to the 40th rugby season is one of the few treasures kept nowadays that proves the date of establishment of the club. This institution is considered the world's oldest club by the Guinness World Records books, as it was the first to have official records of its establishment.

Another rugby club, St. Thomas' Hospital, has records of its founding in 1864.

In 1854, the first Irish club is founded: Dublin University Football Club, better known as Trinity College, member of Dublin University, which keeps extensive documentation that gives credit to its foundation. Dublin University enjoys the privilege of being the oldest in Ireland, established in 1592 by Queen Elizabeth I of England.

In 1857, the first Scottish club is founded in Edinburgh: The Edinburgh Academicals.

Edinburgh Achademicals team

Agreements for playing

It was very usual at that time that the rival teams would not agree on the way to play rugby. That is why the clubs decided to get together to find a single rule book for our sport.

This way, on 26 October 1863, twelve representatives from the clubs and institutions of London schools that practised the sport gathered in the Freemasons' tavern in London in order to establish a universal and definite code. Despite the many meetings, no one was satisfied and there were no agreements regarding the regulations to endorse.

> Out of the twelve clubs that were present in the meetings, some decided to adhere to the rules of the football played at Cambridge University and established the Football Association, which has since then played football following the rules we know nowadays as soccer.

Others refused to sign the agreement and went their own ways, which would years later end in the creation of England's Rugby Union in 1871.

In fact, in 1871, in the Pall Mall restaurant in London, twenty-one English clubs got together and founded the Rugby Football Union (RFU).

Their rules ratified the prohibition of tripping and kicking. And in order to counteract the criticism that this measure provoked, they imposed as a rule one of the most distinctive features of this sport: the tackle.

The statute was quite incomplete.

They did not establish how many players there should be in each team, and because of this, they were still excessive numbers in the practice.

Only in 1875 did universities reduce the number of players to fifteen, which was made official two years later, in 1877, when the national teams for England and Ireland faced off.

The International Rugby Board (IRB)

The lack of agreement among the British countries (the only ones which practised rugby) on the interpretation of the rugby regulations created many conflicts.

England expected to be the supreme authority of the game and the one every other rugby union should obey.

But Scotland, as well as Wales and Ireland, refused to accept the English authority.

To put an end to these arguments, they agreed to build an international committee in 1889, made of members of each country, and whose goal was to write the regulations that would govern the international matches.

This international committee was the first organism that regulated rugby and was called the International Rugby Football Board (IRFB), and later the International Rugby Board (IRB).

As the years went by, many countries which did not have any rugby tradition joined the board as members, and they spread the sport to the distant places in the world.

> At the end of 2014, the IRB changed its named and started to be known as World Rugby.

The referee

At the begining, the referee had little authority and, therefore, his position had a minor importance.

To do their job, they only had a white handkerchief (or a bunting) in his hand, which was waved every time a player committed an infringement. Apart from this, they carried a sanction notebook.

The introduction of the whistle allowed the referee to have an incomparable tool to make himself heard and impose authority during the match. This innovation took place in 1883.

RUGBY EXPANDS

South Africa

Rugby was introduced to South Africa by British colonists and began to be played in the Cape colony around 1875. In 1883, the Stellenbosch club was formed in the predominantly Boer farming district outside Cape Town and rugby was enthusiastically adopted by the young Boer farmers. As British and Boer migrated to the interior they helped spread the game from the Cape colony through the Eastern Cape, and Natal, and along the gold and diamond routes to Kimberley and Johannesburg.

The national team are known as the Springboks. The jersey is a dark myrtle green with a gold collar and a logo of a leaping springbok and a protea.

South Africa have won the World Cup twice, in 1995 in their first appearance when they also hosted the event and again in 2007 in Paris. The 1995 tournament concluded with then President Nelson Mandela, wearing a Springbok jersey and matching baseball cap, presenting the trophy to the South Africa's captain François Pienaar.

Springbok

New Zealand

Rugby was introduced to New Zealand in 1870 by Charles John Monro in Nelson College, and the first rugby match was played against Nelson Football Club on 14 May. A visit to Wellington later that same year resulted in a match between Nelson and Wellington. By the following year, the game had been organized in Wellington, and subsequently rugby was taken up in Wanganui and Auckland in 1873 and Hamilton in 1874. It is thought that by the mid-1870s, the game had been taken up by the majority of the colony.

In 1905 a New Zealand team, who became known as the "Originals", toured the British Isles and France winning all of their games apart from controversially losing the test against Wales. As the team swept through Britain dressed in black jerseys they were christened "All Blacks" by the local press and the public.

New Zealand's national team, commonly referred to as the All Blacks, are the most successful team in international rugby. They won the inaugural Rugby World Cup in 1987. They won its second Rugby World Cup on home soil in 2011, and in 2015 they became the first country to win back to back Rugby World Cups beating Australia 34-17 in the final played at Twickenham, London.

New Zealand silver fern

Australia

In 1863, the first formal rugby football club was formed at Sydney University. In 1869, Newington College was the first Australian school to play rugby in a match against the University of Sydney. From this beginning, the first metropolitan competition in Australia developed, formally beginning in 1874.

Australia's national rugby union team is The Wallabies. They have has won the World Cup on two occasions, in 1991 against England at Twickenham, and then again in 1999 in Wales against France. The team plays in green and gold.

Wallaby

Rugby in Argentina

The beginnings

In 1873, exactly half a century after William Webb Ellis's famous run, rugby arrived in Argentina.

Close to where we can find the Buenos Aires Planetarium nowadays, what is now known as Palermo Woods (Bosques de Palermo), a match took place among some members of the Buenos Aires Cricket Club. That first match was played on 12 June 1873, between Banks and City.

However, for most people, this game is not officially considered the first rugby matched played in Argentina because the rules of this match were a mixture of rugby football and association football rules.

This meeting, far from completing the twenty required players in each team (according to the rules at that time), could only gather twenty-four British enthusiasts. The team from Banks played with eleven men, and the City, with thirteen.

This way, the first rugby match played with the English Union rules took place on 14 May 1874, in Flores Athletic Club, which is located in Caballito neighbourhood.

This first match was played between Mister Trench's and Mister Hogg's sides.

The field was known as the Old Polo Ground and was located in the Buenos Aires's neighbourhood of Caballito, close to the railway, ten blocks away from the current *Ferrocarril Oeste* football club.

This first period in Argentinian rugby is characterised by the British influence in the sport, as rugby was almost exclusively played by British residents.

The founding clubs

10 April 1899 is a very meaningful date because the committee who organised the first rugby championship in the country was formed. It was called The River Plate Rugby Union Championship, a direct precedent of the Argentina Rugby Union.

This committee got together in the offices of a sports magazine called *River Plate Sport & Pastime*, and drew up the bylaws in English. This was because only the British played rugby in Argentina.

Only from 1908 on was it compulsory to use the Spanish language.

There were five clubs that established the Rugby Union:
- Belgrano Athletic Club
- Buenos Aires Football Club
- Flores Athletic Club
- Lomas Athletic Club
- Rosario Athletic Club

Rugby match in Argentina in 1900

Los Pumas

The history of the Pumas starts in 1965. Argentina was going on a long tour to South Africa and Rhodesia (today, Zimbabwe), where they would play sixteen games.

During the tour, a South African journalist from the *Weekly Farmers*, mistook the jaguar on their emblem for a puma. Because of this, the South African press dubbed the Argentina national team the Pumas, a nickname that would remain forever to identify and distinguish Argentina's representatives in rugby.

Due to the great sports results, the tour marked a new stage in the history of rugby in Argentina. Their success was such that from then on, the Argentinian team began to be recognised internationally. This way, they became a reference in the rugby world.

Argentina managed to get on the rugby map of that time, because beyond the victories and defeats, they showed they could play against the most powerful of this sport as equals.

In that historic tour, the team got the desired sports prestige. The initial kick had been given. Since then, he team has been growing slowly but steadily through the years.

Emblem of the Pumas

CHAPTER 2
GETTING TO KNOW RUGBY

THE AIM OF THE GAME

There is something essential that you should know, the engine that gives meaning to every one of the things you do on the field. I am talking about the aim of the game.

It is very important that you know the purpose of this game, as everything you do (running, passing, tackling, kicking, etc.) will lead you directly or indirectly to fulfill this purpose.

I invite you to read a small book called *Laws of the Game [of Rugby Union]*. This book consists of a set of rules that control every aspect of the game (players' clothing, ground sizes, ways of scoring points, allowed actions, forbidden actions, etc.). Be curious, you can read it to clear up your doubts. It is vital that you know very well the regulatory aspects of our sport.

The *Laws of the Game [of Rugby Union]* says:

> The game's objective is to score as many points as possible against an opposing team by carrying, passing, kicking and grounding the ball, according to the laws of the game, its sporting spirit and fair play.

In any sport where there is a ball, this will be the main protagonist and the most valuable object we could possess. That is why it is so important to take care of it.

The ball is an object of desire for every player without distinction, because with it we can run, kick, pass, and let loose all our dreams and imagination.

With a blend of affection for the oval ball, unconditional love towards the game, and great determination, Miguel "Negro" Iglesias, a coach from my club, who was also an example of a rugby man, would always tell us: "There is only one ball and I want to have it." Miguel emphasised with his words the importance of possessing the ball and taking care of it. Because without it, we cannot score tries.

Whoever wants to stand out in the game will have to get the ball, as only by possessing the ball will he be in a position to fulfill the object of the game: scoring points.

Rugby ball

The team which does not have the ball at the start of the game, or which loses it after getting back, only has one way out: fighting to try and regain possession of the ball.

Now, having the ball is only the beginning of a long road; it is only the first step towards the aim of scoring points.

In fact, there is a path which every player has to take in order to achieve this goal. These steps are:

> 1) Getting the ball.
> 2) Keeping it.
> 3) Using it.
> 4) Going forward.

Once the ball is in the team's possession, it has to be kept, but not in any way, because the team that has the ball and keeps it, but goes backwards (that is, away from the opponent's in-goal) is ultimately getting away from it's aim.

Besides, if the player does not play the game with continuity, meaning he does not use the ball, he will not be able to reach the goal.

In rugby, the player (and the team) that does not make use of the ball they have is punished.

The player who throws himself on the floor to get a ball and has no intentions of getting back up, is not making use of the ball, and he is threatening the continuity of the game. In this case, he will be penalised by the referee and, as a consequence, he will lose the ball.

Now that you know the aim or purpose of the game and the path you have to follow to achieve it, I invite you to get to know the technical and regulation aspects that will allow you to fulfil that goal, apart from playing in a safer environment.

LITTLE OVAL DICTIONARY

Rugby is an incredible sport, but also very complex.

It has a terminology that is tiresome but – along the years – we have learnt to understand and love it, since it is part of the roots and traditions of the game.

The experts on the game say that, after chess, rugby is the sport that has the biggest number of combinations possible.

This game comprises a universe of variations which makes it a discipline that can be difficult to understand for any spectator who does not know about this sport.

Furthermore, there is a complexity typical of the language. Most of the words used worldwide are in English due to the origin of this sport. In my country, Argentina, the influence of the English language was so significant that only in 1908 it was decided to draw up the bylaws and regulations in Spanish. But even now, almost two hundred years after the origins of rugby, the English terms dominate the scene: try, in-goal, maul, and ruck are usual words heard in Argentina.

However, my journey through some Spanish speaking countries has allowed me to know some regional expressions that form the idiosyncrasy of every rugby country.

What called most my attention were some expressions used in Spain such as *melé* (scrum), *ensayo* (try), or *placaje* (tackle).

But, apart from the different terms, the complexity of the language is present in every place where rugby is practised.

Here are some basic concepts that may help improve our knowledge about our sport.

Forward pass:
This is a pass executed forward. It is forbidden in our sport and penalised by the referee with a scrum for the opponent.

Knock-on:
This is produced when the player drops the ball forward. In this case, the referee also declares a scrum for the rival team.

Offside:
When a player does not respect the minimum distances established in the regulations, we say he is offside. The referee may award a penalty or a scrum for the team that did not commit the infringement.

In-goal:
This is the area of the field located in both ends, and it is where the players have to ground the ball so as to score a try.

Types of players

In Rugby Union, the team is made up of fifteen players, eight of them are called forwards, and the remaining seven are backs.

> **Forwards:** they are the players who intervene in the battle for the ball in two physical involvement set pieces: scrum and line-out.
>
> **Backs:** these are the players who align themselves behind the two set pieces like scrum or line-out. Their name means 'defenders'.

Scrum

Set pieces

Rugby has a series of formations wich are an essencial and distinctive element as a sport. Some of them are called set pieces because they are executed to restart the game after it has been interrupted. They are:

Scrum: it is the main formation of rugby, as no other discipline in the world has it. It is made by the joining of the eight forwards of each team that, grabbing each other, confront the rival. The goal is to push the opponent so as to get the ball that is thrown into the middle of the tunnel between the two front rows at which point the two hookers can compete for the ball, attempting to hook the ball back in the direction of their team mates.

Lineout: this is used to restart the game after the ball leaves the field. Each team forms a line of players perpendicularly to the outside line (called the touchline). Those lines should stand one metre away from each other. To restart the game, the ball is thrown to the middle of the line so that the forwards can jump and fight for it.

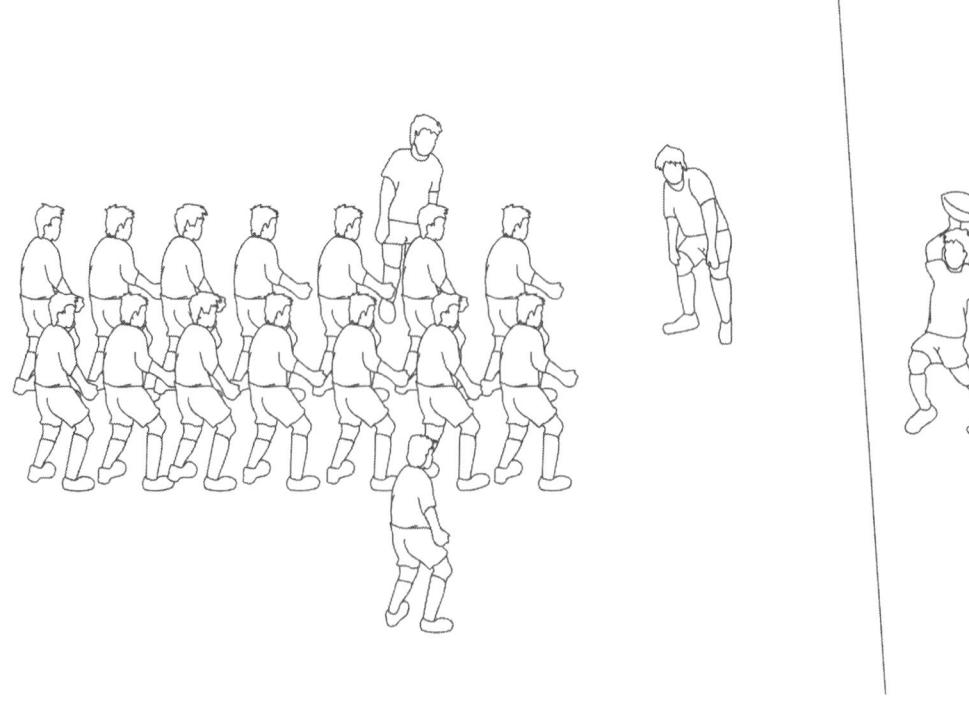

Lineout

Other pieces

Maul: it occurs when the ball carrier is held by one or more opponents and one or more of the ball carrier's team mates holds on (binds) as well (a maul therefore needs a minimum of three players). The ball must be off the ground.

Maul

Ruck: it is formed if the ball is on the ground and one or more players from each team who are on their feet close around it. Players must not handle the ball in the ruck, and must use their feet to move the ball backwards or drive over it so that it emerges at the team's hindmost foot, at which point it can be picked up.

Ruck

Ways of scoring points

Unlike football, in rugby there are many ways of scoring points, whether with the hands or the feet.

Besides, the points value of the scoring has the objective of making rugby an attractive sport with a lot of continuity, encouraging an attacking game.

In the beginnings of rugby, there were no points or scoreboards, given that the team who reached the goal with the ball fulfilled their purpose and, as a result, the game ended.

The game evolved and the points system grew with it, until the system we know today was implemented, with tries, conversions, drop goals, and penalty kicks.

A detail of each one.

Try: it is the most traditional and characteristic way a team has to score points. It consists in grounding the ball inside the opponent's in-goal. It is worth five points.

Penalty try: even without grounding the ball in the rival in-goal, the referee may award a try in the face of imminent scoring frustrated by an infringement by the defending team. That is called a penalty try. It is worth seven points.

Conversion: after every try, the team has an extra prize, the chance to "convert" the try into a goal. It is executed by kicking a ball placed on the ground, in a straight line from the point where the try was grounded. If the ball is kicked over the crossbar and between the goal posts, it is called a conversion and gives the team two extra points (penalty tries score an immediate seven points, with no conversion having to be taken).

Drop goal: it is the way of scoring points by a drop kick. It can be done at any moment during the game. The ball must touch the ground between being dropped and kicked over the crossbar and between the goal posts. It is worth three points.

Penalty goal: it is the way of scoring points by a kick from the ground. It is executed after a serious infringement. The ball must be kicked over the crossbar and between the goal posts. It is worth 3 points.

Types of infringements

Penalty: it is a major infringement. It gives the rival team the chance to kick to the goal posts to score points.

Free-kick: it is a minor infringement, a team may not score points from a free-kick. Its purpose is restarting the game.

Goal posts

There is a very peculiar story around the shape of the rugby goal posts.

Few people know that the current shape displayed by the goal posts is closely related to the traumatic experiences of the beginnings of our sport.

In the 19th century, it was a usual practise that, after a try, the players would position themselves in front of the goal (it was a football goal owing to their common origins) in order to prevent the conversion of the goal. In that period, a try did not award points, only the possibility of converting a goal.

Protected by the laws which did not say anything about it nor penalised it, the players got into the nasty habit of placing themselves in great numbers in front of the goal so that the ball would not get in and thus stopping the conversion of a try into a goal.

As a result, after a short time, players adopted the method of kicking the ball over the crossbar in order to score points. This way, it would not be possible to block the goal and prevent a goal. The H shape was used to guarantee that the ball went over the goal and not on the sides.

The new shape of the goal gave rugby a new boost as it contributed to the growth of the game by improving the quality of the show.

Player getting ready to kick to the goal posts

KNOWING THE LAWS

The laws of rugby is a set of rules that let us know what is the aim of the game, as well as what we can and cannot do.

It is very important to know the rules that govern and regulate our sport because this will help us play better and enjoy the game. But most meaningful yet is that knowing the regulations contributes to the players' physical safety.

The regulations of age grade rugby consist of twenty-six rules on different aspects, in which topics such as the duration of the matches, the number of players, special situations in the game, and the *third half* among others are regulated.

The objectives set by the regulations are:

1. Use the game of rugby as a means of formation, recreation, and education.

2. Respect the rights of the boys and girls to a safe, calm, and fun sports practice.

3. Adjust the game to the boys' and girls' maturation levels.

4. Spread the game through the use of easy-to-learn laws.

5. Adapt the teaching to the demands of the game, developing it progressively.

6. Encourage the decision making, the game skills, and the tactical intelligence.

7. Motivate the players, based on the loyalty that the laws of the game demand, to score the highest number possible of points, carrying, passing, kicking, and grounding the ball.

What shouldn't we do?

- We should not tackle a player without the intention of getting hold of him or her.
- We should not tackle the player who, looking to receive a kick, is in the air.
- We should not collapse a maul, as it is very dangerous.
- We should not tackle the player who is pushing in the maul.
- We should not tackle over the chest.
- We should not hand off another player with our closed fist.
- We should not touch or grab the ball in the ruck.

Did you know that the Underage Rugby regulations say that…?

Players can go up one category higher than their age dictates to keep mates and/or friends together, or to strengthen a division with a small number of players.

The kids taking part in a match or training session should not have an age difference bigger than two years according to their birthdate.

The players of the team that plays the ball in the line-out must jump without assistance, either as a support or raising them.

Up until U13, hand-off is allowed but not on the neck, face or head.

The ball carrier is not allowed to run towards the defender with the intent of causing the use of the hand-off.

The coach can cancel the meeting when the weather conditions entail a significant health and/or safety risk for the players.

Except in the U14 category, it is forbidden in all other categories to play a quick start five metres away from the goal line.

In no case can the player receiving a kick from air be tackled until he is on his feet and has started his run.

The player carrying the ball has to try to avoid other players by running, passing the ball or kicking it to the defending team empty spaces, and is not allowed to charge the defending player intentionally. The point of this law is to prevent the players from using physical contact as the only way of attacking.

TECHNICAL HANDBOOK

Rugby is a very difficult and complex sport for many reasons:

- Many players in each team.
- Players with different roles and physical characteristics.
- A lot of skills to teach.
- Difficult and changing laws.
- A ball that bounces in any direction.

This situation means that we need a gradual learning process. It requires time and a plan to be learnt in a better way.

Just as behaviours need a long period of time to become habits, skills are not acquired quickly or magically. We have to take it step by step. It is impossible to learn everything at the same time.

So as not to overwhelm you with difficult stuff, I give you a brief guide with the way of exercising what we call skills, which are important for our game.

These are:

1. The pass

A team that has not developed good passing skills will not be in a position to keep possession of the ball.

Many times there is a wrong concept of the pass. The player who is not marked has to run with the ball in his hands. He should only pass the ball when he cannot keep running with it or when a teammate is in a better position than him to continue the attack and move forward.

Requirements for a good pass

1) Easy to catch

    The perfect pass is the one who goes in a suitable speed, the correct height (hip level) and is heading in front of the receiver. If it has these three elements, then it will easy to catch for the receiver.

2) Neutralise the opponen

    A ball-carrier that executes his pass well (whichever type of pass it is) should be capable of neutralising the opponent so that he cannot continue with his defensive task.

Fixing the defender is what allows us to attract our rival and neutralise his defensive action, so that our supporting receiver has better chances to continue attacking. The carrier has to aim at the opposite side of the defender to where he will pass the ball in order to involve him in the action and neutralise him so that he cannot move off him and on to the receiver.

Passing the ball

3) Right time and place

For the pass to be good, it should not be only technically correct, but also executed with the right timing (not before, not after) and be directed not to any supporting receiver but the one who represents the best option to continue the attack.

2. How to catch the ball

We can receive it from a pass or from the air.

How should we receive it from a pass?
With open hands pointing to the ball.
Bent elbows.
The leg further from the ball also bent.
The arms should be pointing to the ball, but not rigid, so as to absorb the impact.
Catch the ball with your fingertips, because it is there where you have more control and sensibility.

Player catching the ball

How should we catch the ball from a kick?

Do not lose sight of the ball at any moment. This means keeping an eye on it at all times, since its departure, until it is caught.

Bring your arms up at head height, fingers pointing up and form a cradle with your arms. This allows the ball not to escape between the elbows, which should be parallel.

Get side-on the direction of play, with your chest facing sideways and your leading hand towards the ball, grip it and take it on your side. This has logical reasons. Firstly, if the ball is dropped it will go backwards rather than knocked on, and secondly, to offer the rival the strong part of your body –your shoulders and thighs–, protecting your weaker and more vulnerable areas.

Press the ball to your chest.

Turn around to shield the ball. Turning your back to the opposition allows you to move the ball away from the adversary and avoid a battle.

Player receiving the ball from the air

SEBASTIÁN PERASSO   67

3. How to pick up the ball

There are three basic conditions to to pick up the ball correctly. These are:
- Knees bent.
- Fingers spread and under the ball.
- Grabbing it from the side.

Bending your knees allows you to keep your hips no higher than your shoulders, which helps take the ball fairly and provides a bigger reach to the hands.

Grabbing the ball from the side helps so there are fewer chances of kicking it or tripping over your own feet.

Player picking up the ball from the ground

Lastly, positioning yourself on your side means showing your stronger flank to the opponent and protecting the weakest and most fragile parts of your body from them.

The best method to pick up the ball while running is to pick it up with a hand from behind the ball, so that the other hand will simply act as a guide from the front.

4. Fall on the ball

Falling on the ball

Along with the skill to pick up the ball, we are rarely taught how to fall on to ball. However, many matches are lost because of the lack of skills in this aspect of the game.

But even worse is that not only the spectators but even the players and coaches tend to put down a loss to bad luck when, actually, it is a consequence of the lack of these skills.

There are some key factors that are part of the ability to fall on the ball and without those it would be impossible to properly execute it. These are:

Movement:

When a player is running back, he should first slide his feet towards the ball and catch it from above with his arm to secure it. Besides, he should always have his back to the rivals in order to protect the ball.

It is very important to go full speed to get the ball, but in the final metres, we should reduce the speed to achieve coordination and better control of our movements.

Securing it:

Once the ball has been taken, we should press it to out chest to secure it.

Getting up:

The player should get up immediately to allow the continuity of the game, otherwise the referee will award a free kick against him.

5. The tackle

The tackle is one of the most distinctive features of our sport. It is a complex technique because it has many key factors.
They are:

- Straight back to give off strength.
- Chin up to avoid the contact with the boots of the tackled player.

Tackle

- Leg thrust to give greater strength to the tackle.
- Arms firmly closed to use them like pincers.
- Body crouched for the impact.

Tackle only when you feel sure and after having practised it a lot of times.

6. Running

There are four ways of running with the ball so as to break the defence and try to advance on the field:

> Side step
> Swerve step
> Hand off
> Dummy

Side step

It implies suddenly running towards the defender's opposite side and constitutes one of the most widely used evasion techniques.

There are certain factors that make for a good technique.

Side step

Firstly, we should get to the spot with short steps in order to choose the exact place for the side step.

Secondly, all our body's weight should fall on the leg that will boost us and we should pick up speed after doing it.

Lastly, after doing this, the player should try to straighten his run and resume his original path.

Swerve step

It entails running on the outside of the defender.

The essential thing is to trick the defender by making him believe that we are going to run on his inside shoulder and then, when the defender is still, we run on his outside shoulder.

We should cross our legs and form a small arch with the imaginary line of our path.

Hand-off

Hand-off

The hand off implies moving the defender with our hand. There are certain aspects that make for a good hand-off technique.

Our arm should be bent to use it as a lever and get away from the tackler by giving us a boost, and our hand which is on the defender should be open.

Dummy

It consists in making the defender move. The dummy is the evasion technique in which the one who moves is the defender and not the ball carrier.

It is important to complete the whole technical movement of the pass and even make the gestures to trick the defender.

Player executing the dummy

DEVELOPING GOOD HABITS

This is a short list of behaviours which are necessary to encourage and promote so that they can be used as valuable tools in your learning process.

Go forward.
Look for the gaps in the defence.
Carry the ball with both hands.
Crouch so as to keep the centre of gravity low.
Keep the ball away from the rival.
Stay on your feet.
Fall and present the ball.
Have a supportive attitude.
Tackle and get up immediately.
Look forward.
Have a good communication with your teammates.
Know the laws.
Pick up the ball form the ground by the side, not by the front.

THE PRINCIPLES OF THE GAME

I have mentioned that rugby is a game of great complexity. For you to understand this sport in an easy way, I will list and explain the principles of the game.

The four principles of rugby:

> **Go forward**
> **Support**
> **Continuity**
> **Pressure**

Go forward

It is the basic principle of the game and the most important one. That is why it is crucial to practise this since we are young.

> The player has to go forward with the ball. Straight runs, parallel to the touch lines, are the ones that make you advance, and they give the ball carrier the possibility of having supporting mates.

Finding the gaps is the key to being able to go forward.

Support

Player supporting the ball-carrier

One of the universal principles of rugby is the support, as rugby is a game of support. This affirmation is based on two truths as old as rugby itself.

In the first place, no player has the ball in his hands for longer than a minute during the game, if we consider a rugby union match that lasts eighty minutes.

In the second place, only one is the carrier and the remaining teammates are potential supporters.

This shows the importance of developing the sense of support and at the same time, learning the techniques and skills that are useful for the different supports to work properly.

These three aspects are key for a good support:

- Attitude
- Skills
- Stamina

It is necessary that the players remain in the game once they let go of the ball. If we pass the ball and forget about the game, it is difficult to get the ball again.

Many players mistakenly believe that all they have to do is to pass the ball, but, actually, that is the moment when their task starts, when they pass the ball.

The supportive task is as decisive as the task of the ball-carrier.

> A good support is characterised by being:
> - Open
> - Deep
> - Perpendicular to the in-goal

The open support helps the creation of gaps in the defence. If there is more space among the defenders, there are more gaps through which we can escape.

Besides, the support should be deep because otherwise, one support would conceal another.

Lastly, a support should be perpendicular to the in-goal, which means they have to run in a straight line.

Continuity

What does continuity mean? It means keeping the ball moving. There is continuity when the attack does not stop.

In rugby, the team that has the ball in it's possession needs to use it. The laws of the game do not allow to waste time with the ball (like in football). Not using the ball means losing continuity.

The player that drops to the ground to catch the ball and stays on the ground with it does not provide continuity to the game, so the referee can penalise him and take the ball possession from him.

When the ball is caught up between many players and cannot get out, the referee can also stop the game, otherwise the game cannot have continuity.

Pressure

Pressure is a vital element for every defending team. If we do not put up pressure, we are not going to get the ball back.

Pressure is the ideal way to take away time and space from the attacker.

> Without the time to think, the attacker will make worse decisions.
> Without space, the attacker will have less variables where to attack.

Pressure defence

SAFETY

Physical safety

Rugby is a contact sport. This means that brushes and hits (always according to what the laws regulate) are something usual.

For this reason, you should ensure your own physical safety and integrity as well as that of your teammates and your rivals.

Managing to reduce the injuries to a minimum is everyone's commitment and duty, and that requires taking care of everyone.

Respecting the rules is one of the conditions for the sport activity to be the least dangerous possible.

Some advice that will contribute to your safety:

> Wear a gumshield.
> Wear rugby boots, rugby socks and a rugby shirt.
> Make sure your laces are always tied.
> Do not wear necklaces of any type around your neck.
> Respect the resting periods according to the age garde.
> Have a doctor present during games.
> Drink water and stay hydrated during the match.

Affective safety

There is no doubt that the context surrounding the players benefits or hinders the teaching process.

Every one of us has to help create the suitable setting or atmosphere so that everyone can enjoy rugby and learn.

How do we achieve affective safety? Through the care, support, respect and affection given to each one of the players.

Creating the conditions to practise rugby in a harmonious and enjoyable setting has to be a commitment made not only by the coach but also by all the players.

When do we threaten the emotional safety of the others?

1. When we compare

Comparison can represent a blow to your mates' self-esteem. We have to accept the other kids with their differences.

2. When we lie

If we lie, we put at risk something as important as the trust that other people have put on us.

3. When we do not get involved

If we do not pay attention, if we are distracted, and do not get involved in the activity we are participating in, not only are we incorrectly fulfilling our task, but we are also distracting our teammates. This disconnection with reality has a contagious effect on the rest. Be careful.

4. When we are disinterested

Our disinterest in what we are doing creates a climate which is unsuitable for learning. Never lose your enthusiasm.

CHAPTER 3
GUARDIANS OF THE GAME

THE SPIRIT OF RUGBY

You have probably heard many times about the spirit of rugby, and you may not know what that expression means.

As rugby is a contact sport, in which there are brushes, collisions, and physical contact, it was necessary that, apart from what the laws say, there should be a series of good habits that would regulate the behaviour of the players as well as the coaches, referees, and spectators. These good habits so essential for the health of the game have to do with the spirit of rugby.

Rugby exceeds what it means to play, because rugby **is its laws but also its spirit**. This spirit has been guarded and passed down from generation to generation until our time.

> The spirit of the game is the flame which lights the road of rugby, which guides it through time like a compass that leads new generations to safe port.

We cannot see it, but we know it exists and it is always present. The challenge, then, is to keep it alive.

In rugby, the spirit reflects loyalty, correctness, and chivalry; it reveals nobility in victory, and also correctness and good manners in defeat.

The spirit of the game is generosity, limitless dedication, and commitment.

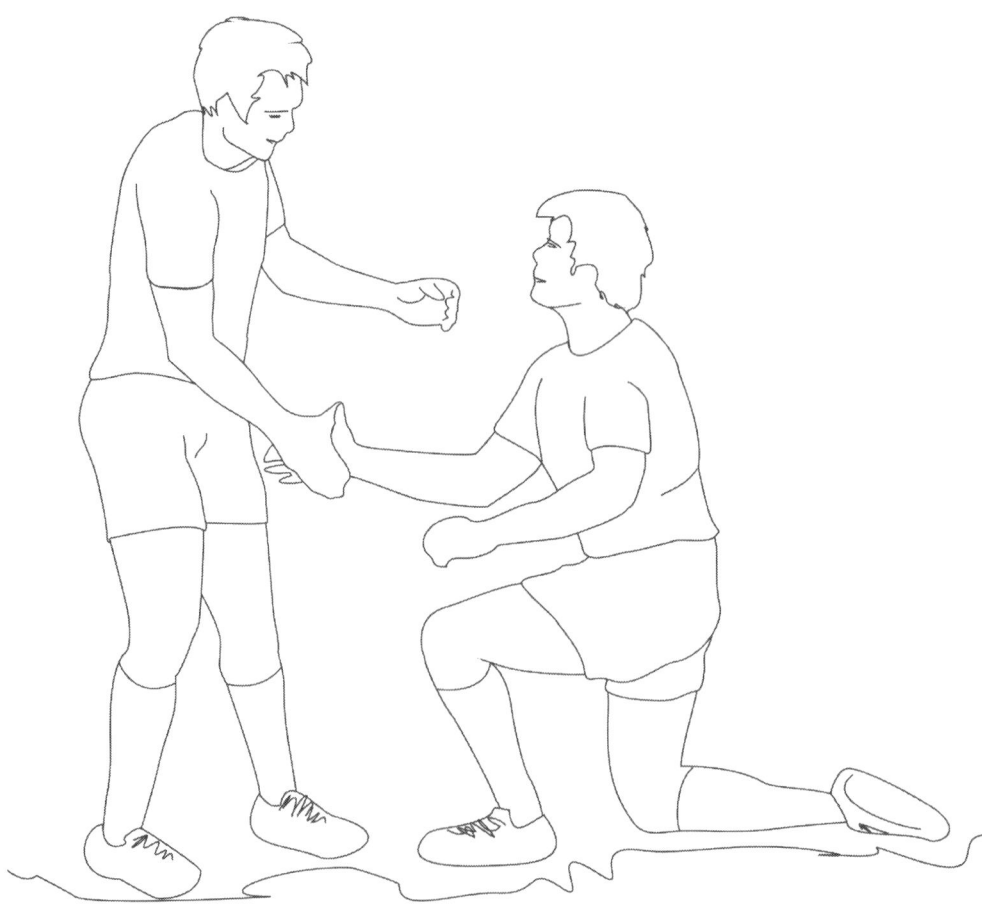

Greeting the opponent

The spirit does not recognise differences and does not notice races or nationalities. It is only one and makes everyone equal. It is what allows the players to understand each other and manage to speak the same language in spite of the native language each team may speak. The spirit is that magic potion of understanding that allows to shorten distances, break down barriers, and unite the whole family of rugby in one direction.

There are certain behaviours that are not in the laws but are very beneficial and healthy to carry out. These behaviours feed and uplift the spirit of rugby. Some of these are:

- Help the fallen player get up.
- Protect the player when there is risk of injury.
- Greet the rivals when the game has ended.
- Applaud good actions.
- Help a teammate ground a try.
- Do not mock the opponent.
- Stay to share the "third half".

THE TRUE SPORTSPERSON

The first thing we should specify is who the true sportsperson is. A sportsperson is not the one who practises a sport, but the one who, apart from practising it, has learnt:

- To supress his fury, his anger.
- To be tolerant towards his teammates.
- Not to cheat.
- To win fairly.

There are more than six million players around the world. The game has spread in such a way that rugby is practised in one hundred and nineteen countries in the world. This constitutes a reason why everyone should be proud, as it is very positive that so many children and youngsters practise our favourite sport.

> But... what good would it do to have so many oval ball players if they do not behave the way the sport demands? It would be a total failure and it would prove that sport is not useful to be a better person.

The challenge is, then, to try to be true sportspeople.

The true sportsperson is the one who treats his opponents respectfully, the one who makes humility and correctness his standard. It is the one who, thanks to the practise of the sport, feel like a better person every day.

It is always said that rugby is a school of values. The school of rugby hopes you are the best students. Let's get to it!

Five actions we should never forget:

- Greet the rival.
- Accept the referee's calls.
- Do your best.
- Applaud good actions.
- Take part in the third half.

Five actions we should avoid:

- Arrive late at an appointment.
- Forget your gumshield.
- Not pay attention.
- Say bad words.
- Disobey the rules.

MY BEHAVIOUR

We should be humble, because even the word winner we owe to the losers.

When each one of you puts on a rugby shirt, you are not alone anymore, you start being part of something so great and sacred as the big family of rugby.

This way, as rugby players, you begin to be the most important.

But what does it mean to be important? It means that you are the most valuable thing of this sport but at the same time you have a responsibility to the game you have chosen.

Because of this, everything you do, every movement, every attitude, and every behaviour, as small as it is or looks, is not irrelevant.

What should we be like?

- Respectful.
- Well-mannered.
- Selfless.
- Generous.
- Humble.

Respectful:

Respect is the foundation of good cohabitation and the most important value we can put into practice. Respect as a value plays a crucial role in our lives, not only in sports and the things related to it.

It is the essence of human relationships, of life in community, of teamwork, and of any interpersonal relationship.

Many times respect is mistaken with good manners or kindness, but respect is much more than all that. Respect is an attitude.

We owe that attitude to everybody (coaches, teammates, rivals), and also to the things around us, like the training material or our own clothing, for example. If we did not take care of our belongings (shirt, gumshield, boots), we would not be respecting something which in some way we associate with. We would not appreciate their worth and the effort it took to get them.

Besides, respect includes many characteristics, as punctuality, humility, and correctness; it is healthy coexistence and fair competition; it is honourability, courtesy, and correctness in victory, as well as nobility and recognition in defeat.

Respect everyone and everything, and you will certainly be respected. That is the basic rule for any sport coexistence.

Well-mannered:

In rugby, manners are a synonym for self-control, meaning that the person can control itself regardless of the circumstances.

A well-mannered person is the one who, whether he wins or loses, keeps his good manners.

Rugby is a contact game, of constant friction. In this sense, it is determining that the ones who practise it are well-mannered. Otherwise, it would be impossible to play according to the values required by this sport.

When are we not well-mannered?

- When we do not know how to behave.
- When we act in bad faith.
- When we lose control.
- When we fake or cheat.
- When we do not respect the authority of the referee.

Selfless:

In this game, we find difficulties with every step we take.

The rugby player has to develop a spirit of selflessness because, without effort, it will be impossible to reach any goal.

Selflessness implies getting rid of selfish behaviours. Selflessness as a value means knowing how to set aside our comforts, our usually lazy actions in order to be in the service of the others.

Many times you will have to choose between your likes, your interests, and your comfort and the team's interests. Here is where we show our spirit of selflessness.

Selflessness means that the benefit of the team is above my own interests. Selflessness is commitment to the other, improvement, perseverance, and a vocation to service.

Generous:

You may not know this, but rugby is the sport with the highest number of players in each team. There are fifteen players on each side.

Only Australian football exceeds this number, with eighteen players per team, a sport only practised in Australia.

This means that, unlike any other sport, you will always have a lot of teammates by your side. And it also means that you will not get anything on your own.

Can we play as if we were alone then? Impossible. If we do not work together and as a team, our chances of success and enjoyment will be reduced.

The word *mate* comes from a Middle Low German word meaning 'comrade' and is related to meat, with the underlying concept of eating together. We have to know and understand that our teammates are precisely mates because we share something with them (our time, a joke, a third half, a team, a club) and that if we stop acting as a part of the team, so will the rest.

I invite you to share everything, and thus, treat the others as true mates.

Humble:

Humility is an everyday behaviour, a way of being, a way of life. Humility is one of the noblest virtues.

Being humble does not mean being weak; actually, it means just the opposite. Being humble is a sign of great strength, not weakness.

Humility makes us tolerant towards a result, and patient towards our peers. Besides, it creates a calm and peaceful atmosphere.

> If we are humble:
>
> - We admit our mistakes.
> - We accept the rival's superiority.
> - We admit we can win or lose.
> - We acknowledge that the rival has been better.
> - We admit we have to improve.
> - We forgive our own mistakes.

If we are proud and arrogant towards the others, we will stop being humble, and most serious and fateful aspect of this is that we will certainly lose the esteem and affection of our teammates and our rivals.

> *Foundations of behaviour*
> Keep in mind that:
>
> - Respect is the foundation of cohabitation.
> - Honesty is the foundation of trust.
> - Humility is the foundation of growth.
> - Generosity is the foundation of friendship.
> - Tolerance is the foundation of harmony.
> - Commitment is the foundation of progress.

15 TIPS FOR THE RUGBY PLAYER

1 - A rugby player never puts his personal interests or needs before those of the team.

2 - A rugby player enjoys contact and hits, because they make him stronger.

3 - A rugby player does not hit back, he tackles back; he does not insult or attack back, he ignores it.

4 - A rugby player does not ask for anything, he gives his all.

5 - A rugby player does not need the ball to enjoy the game.

6 - A rugby player never talks about himself, and even less about his virtues.

7 - A rugby player never looks for the most comfortable situation for him, but the most favourable one for his team.

8 - A rugby player feels uncomfortable when complimented.

9 - A rugby player knows that success is the internal peace we feel when we are sure we have done our best.

10 - A rugby player values effort and selflessness much more than talent.

11 - A rugby player respects and values the strength of his rivals.

12 - A rugby player learns more from defeats than from victories.

13 - A rugby player is harder and stricter on himself than on any other.

14 - A rugby player does not protest, does not complain, does not make excuses.

15 - A rugby player never asks for a break, never quits, never gives up.

THE 10 REASONS OF A TEAM

The ten reasons which show that a team has been formed are:

1 - When the players put themselves in second place and sacrifice their personal interests for the benefit of the collective interests.

2 - When a defeat brings about disappointment and sadness, but not anger or rage.

3 - When the players' hugs and pep talks happen at the end of the match, and not before it.

4 - When individualities are raised and strengthened and complement each other.

5 - When there are no reproaches or grudges in the face of a sports setback.

6 - When the criticism towards the group is always constructive and not destructive.

7 - When every match is a lesson learnt.

8 - When all the players pursue the same goals and have identical dreams.

9 - When generosity, commitment, and enthusiasm defeat selfishness and disinterest.

10 - When, after the match, the players can look each other in the eyes without any reproaches.

Team huddled together

CHAPTER 4
WINNING AND LOSING

"Sometimes you win and sometimes you lose, but the important thing is that there is always something to learn."
Anonymous

Winning

You know this very well. When you first start playing and practising a sport, you know beforehand that there are three possible outcomes: winning, drawing, or losing.

As coaches, we want you to live each match with joy and enthusiasm, whichever the result. Today, that is meaningless and unimportant. Our objective is that each one of you can enjoy the game and that this serves as an educational setting at the same time.

But apart from the message we pass on every day, everyone has a competitive spirit, and it makes sense that you would want to win and show that you are good and better than the rest.

Remember that everyone, absolutely everyone, is going to win and lose. What is important is how you react to that. It is essential that you learn to win and lose, respecting the opponent and without cheating.

The ones who really know how to win never humiliate the defeated and present an image of discretion, care, simplicity, modesty, and humility.

Winning means knowing how to recognise the effort made by the opponent, respecting them, congratulating them, and acknowledging their feat in the competition. Winning with correctness and without excesses is the best way to respect the rival, because without them there would be no match.

Success is not in the result but the possibility you have of enjoying, learning, growing, making friends, and living this stage in your childhood free from anger and responsibilities.

> **What is winning?**
>
> Winning is never giving up.
> Winning is not feeling defeated.
> Winning is outdoing ourselves.
> Winning is enjoying everything we do.
> Winning is respecting our teammates and our rivals.
> Winning is sharing our dreams with others.
> Winning is making many friends.
> Winning is giving our best.
> Winning is growing as a person.
> Winning is being more confident and having a higher self-esteem.
> Winning is feeling happy.

Losing

Losing is a necessary part of sports and we cannot escape from it because it is part of life itself.

The attitude we have in the face of defeat will make us better or worse people. Do not face defeat as a scandal or a frustration, but as a teaching or a lesson.

When do we lose?

When we get bored.
When we fight.
When we do not show respect.
When we cheat.
When we do not do our best.
When we betray.
When we do not accept defeat.
When we get angry.
When we argue with the referee.
When we do not have a positive attitude.
When we are selfish.

"The important thing in life is not victory but combat; it is not to have vanquished but to have fought well."
                              Pierre de Coubertin

EPILOGUE

CHASING OUR DREAMS

Dear kids, we have reached the end of this road. I thank you for reading this book, and say goodbye with a small reflection.

You have the privilege of childhood. You can enjoy a stage that is meaningful as well as unique, lacking any great responsibilities.

Enjoy as much as you can and never lose your cheek, your simplicity, and your authenticity.

Do not doubt that in rugby you will find a space of support, where you can let your dreams loose and feel whole, safe, and valued.

Run, enjoy, make mistakes, because that is inevitable! But always go forward. Do not give up and never stop making the effort. That giant player we have to knock down. Training in the bitter cold. Or getting up really early to play.

Rugby teaches us there is nothing easy about it. Rugby shapes our character. Nothing is easy to get. But how nice is it when we get it! The joy is incomparable. Let's go look for it without making excuses or giving up.

Rugby teaches us that we cannot get anything alone. If we do not work together as a team, our goals will be harder to reach.

Setting our likes and our interests aside and working together in search of an objective. Another nice lesson rugby gives us which we can apply on our lives.

The ball was put in motion and the match has started.

Do not leave anything undone. Take initiative and be passionate about what you do. You cannot go forward without enthusiasm.

Your instinct will guide you on your way. Let your imagination fly and do not waste time pleasing others o living someone else's life.

If you want to fulfil your dreams, you have to give your everything, do not hold anything back. Do not hesitate. Every dream can be realised if you are willing to chase them with passion and determination.

Some people think rugby belongs only to the winners. I say that this wonderful game belongs to everybody.

Only some can be "the best," but undoubtedly each one of you will be able to be better.

Predict where the ball will bounce; build friendships and dreams, because no one can take away your right to dream.

Never push the game aside, as in it you will always have a shelter, a supportive place. Rugby has to be your home, and the club, the family you have chosen.

When your childhood ends, a cheeky smile will escape your lips; a genuine grin will appear on your face, and you will remember your childhood with a joyful nostalgia.

Rugby will have played its part. That kid who enjoyed his childhood has a lot of joyful and magical moments engraved in his heart.

Play, have fun, feel happy, and at the same time, check, as if by magic, that while we grow with rugby, we are better people than we were before.

Rugby is for everyone

Printed by Amazon Italia Logistica S.r.l.
Torrazza Piemonte (TO), Italy